New Testament Stories

NEW TESTAMENT BIBLE STORIES

as told by Carol Mullan • illustrated by Dan Waring

GOLDEN PRESS
Western Publishing Company, Inc.
® Racine, Wisconsin

ISBN 0-307-10502-4

Third Printing, 1979

Elisabeth and Zacharias were sad. They had prayed many times for children. But they didn't have any, and now they were old. Then an angel came to Zacharias in the temple and told him that their prayers were answered. Elisabeth was going to have a baby, who was to be named John. John was going to be a very special prophet. He would help people to get ready for Jesus, the Savior.

Zacharias wanted to believe the angel, but when he thought about how old he and his wife were, he doubted the angel's words. Because he did not believe what the angel had said, he was no longer able to speak. Whenever he wanted to say anything, he had to write it down.

When the baby was born, the neighbors and relatives thought he should be named Zacharias, after his father. But Zacharias remembered what the angel had said, and he wrote that the baby's name was to be John. When Zacharias finished writing, he was able to talk again. He told the neighbors and relatives that John was going to be a special prophet. How excited they were to learn that the Savior was soon to come to them and that John would help them to get ready for him!

Jesus went from place to place, telling people how they must live while on earth, in order to please God and to live with him in heaven after they died. With power given to him by his heavenly Father, Jesus healed the sick people who came to him believing that he could help them.

Jesus knew that he wouldn't be on earth very long, so he chose twelve men to be his special helpers, called apostles. Putting his hands on the head of each apostle, Jesus gave each one the power to heal sick people in his name. He also prepared them to teach people, just as he did.

Sometimes the apostles did not understand very well. Once they asked Jesus which of his disciples, or followers, was the most important. Jesus called a little child to him and told the apostles that the one who was most important would be as obedient and trusting and loving as the little child in front of them.

Jesus knew that the apostles didn't understand, because another time, when little children were brought to Jesus to be blessed, the apostles tried to send them away. Jesus again explained how important little children are to God. Then Jesus took all of the children in his arms, one by one, and blessed them.

Jesus and his apostles often walked many, many miles over hot, dusty roads in order to teach people. When they finally stopped to eat and rest for the night, they were tired. Their feet were dirty because the roads were full of dust.

One night, after fastening a towel around himself, Jesus filled a basin with water and began to wash the apostles' feet. The apostles were astonished at first; they didn't know what to think. Then they felt ashamed to have Jesus wash their feet. He was the Savior of the world, and the Savior shouldn't be washing their feet, they thought.

Jesus told them not to be ashamed of doing anything to help people. Just as he was helping them, they should help each other.

People often came from far away to listen to Jesus. One day, when the people had listened many hours and it was almost night, Jesus knew that they must be hungry. He asked his apostles if anyone had brought anything to eat. Andrew told Jesus that there was a young boy who had five loaves of bread and two small fish. But that was not very much food to share with five thousand people.

While the apostles had the people sit in groups of fifty, the boy gladly gave his bread and fish to Jesus to share with the people. Jesus looked toward heaven and blessed the food, and as he divided it among the apostles, there was plenty. The apostles passed the food to all the people, and everyone ate until he was full.

Jesus loved to tell stories that helped people to understand what they must do to be better. One story helped them to understand that God loved them, even if they were bad, but that he was happiest when they stopped being bad and, by being good, came back to him.

The story Jesus told was about a man who had two sons. The younger son asked his father for the money he was supposed to get when he was older. He took the money and went to a faraway country, where he spent it all on parties and foolish things.

When his money was gone, the younger son had to work as a servant, feeding pigs. There was a famine in that faraway country, and the younger son never had enough to eat. He thought about how nice it had been to live at home with his father and his older brother.

Deciding he would rather be a servant for his father than starve where he was, the younger son went home to ask his father to forgive him and hire him as a servant. But when his father saw him coming, he ran eagerly to meet him. Then the father had a big dinner prepared to celebrate his younger son's return.

The older son didn't understand why his father was so happy to see the younger son. The father explained that he was happy because the younger son had stopped doing bad things and had come home to him.

Jesus warned people that just listening to his teachings would not get them to heaven. They would have to believe in him and do what he taught them to do if they were to live in heaven with God after they died.

If they obeyed him, he explained, they would be like the wise man who built his house upon a big rock. When the storm came, the wise man didn't have to worry, because his house was safe.

But the people who didn't obey him, Jesus went on, would be like the foolish man who built his house upon sand. When the storm came, his house fell apart.

Sometimes Jesus taught people by asking them questions.

One time he told them to pretend they had a hundred sheep. If one of the sheep were lost, he asked them, wouldn't they leave their other sheep in order to find the lost one? And when they found it, wouldn't they tell their friends and neighbors, so that the friends and neighbors could be happy about it, too?

Jesus wanted the people to understand that, just as the one lost sheep was important to them, each one of them was important to him. He loved each and every one of them.

A neighbor, Jesus explained, is not just someone who lives near you. A neighbor is someone who is happy when you are happy and sad when you are sad. A real neighbor helps you when you are in trouble. Everyone should be a good neighbor, Jesus said. To help people to understand what a good neighbor does, he told this story:

A Jew was going from Jerusalem to Jericho, when thieves beat him and robbed him and left him to die by the side of the road. A priest went by, and so did a Levite. Both men lived near the man, but neither stopped to help him.

Then a Samaritan saw him. Although the Jews and the Samaritans were enemies, this Samaritan bandaged the wounds of the Jew. Then, putting the wounded man on his own donkey, the Samaritan took him to an inn. The Samaritan even paid the innkeeper to take care of the man until he felt better.

Though he lived much farther from the Jew than did the priest or the Levite, the Samaritan was the real neighbor to him.

People knew that Jesus could heal those who were sick, but sometimes the crowds around him were so large that the sick people could not get close enough to ask his help.

One woman had been sick for twelve years. She had gone to many doctors, but no one could help her. When she saw Jesus, she squeezed through the crowd until she could reach out and touch his clothing.

Jesus felt some of his healing power leave him, and he turned around to see who had touched him. He told the woman that she was healed because she believed in him.

Because God was Jesus' father, Jesus had power over death. Three days after he had died, Jesus was resurrected — his spirit went back into his body, and he would never die again.

Even though Jesus had taught people about life after death, he knew that they didn't understand. Not even the apostles really understood, until Jesus went to see them after he was resurrected. Jesus talked with the apostles. He ate a piece of fish and some honey to show them that he truly was alive. And he told them to touch him, so they would know that what they heard and saw was real.

Jesus stayed with the apostles for a while, and then he went to heaven to live with his heavenly Father.

The apostles wanted to tell everyone about Jesus. They were glad when great crowds of people came from near and far for a feast called the Feast of Pentecost.

The apostles didn't know how to speak in all the different languages of the people who came for the feast. But, as the apostles started to tell the people about Jesus, each person who listened to them understood—in his own language—what the apostles were saying.

Many, many people became disciples of Jesus that day.

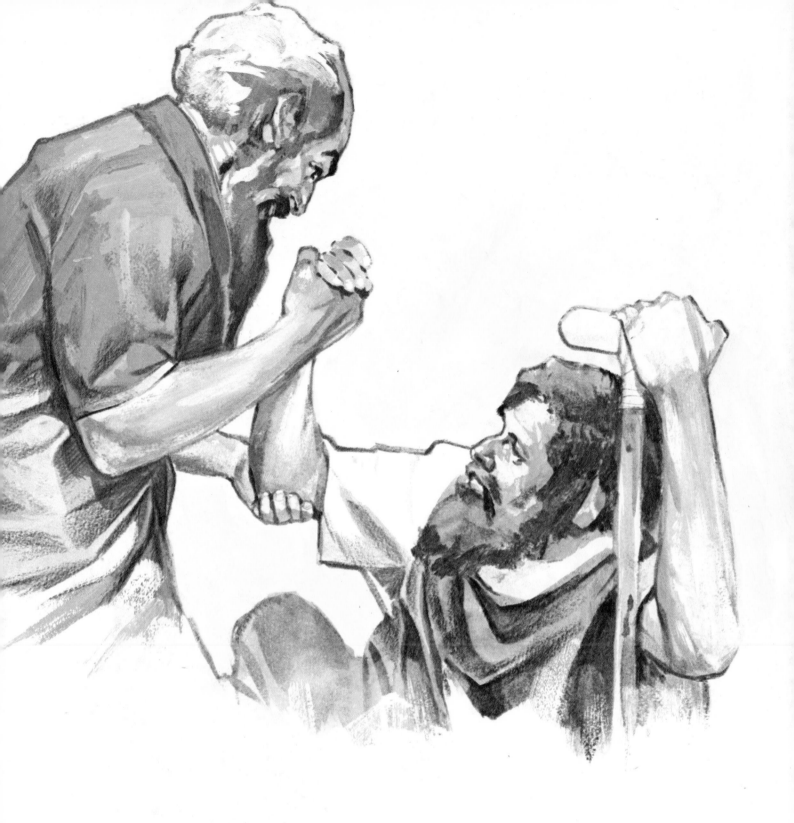

Peter and John, two of Jesus' apostles, went to the temple in Jerusalem to pray. As they came to the gate of the temple, they saw a man begging for money. The man had been crippled all his life and couldn't walk.

Peter didn't have any money, but he gave the beggar something better than money. Telling him that he was being healed in Jesus' name, Peter took the man by his right hand and helped him up.

The man was so happy to be healed that he ran and leaped about. Then he went into the temple with Peter and John to praise God.

From the time he was a little boy in Cilicia, Paul had obeyed the laws of Moses. He thought that Jesus and his disciples were teaching people to disobey the laws of Moses, so he tried to get them thrown into prison.

When Paul was going to Damascus with some other men, to find more of Jesus' disciples to put into prison, a very bright light suddenly shone all around him. The light was so bright that Paul was blinded, and he fell to the ground. Then he heard Jesus' voice asking him why he was hurting the disciples.

Once he understood that Jesus was the Savior that Moses had written about, Paul realized that he had been harming good people. Paul was sorry, and he wanted to know what he could do to help Jesus.

Jesus told him to go on to Damascus. The men who were with Paul led him to the house of a man named Judas. Three days later, Ananias, a disciple, came to him. Ananias told Paul that Jesus had sent him; then he put his hands on Paul's head and blessed him so that he could see again.

Paul was baptized right away. Then he went to Rome and Greece and many other places, to tell as many people as he could about Jesus.

Cornelius was an officer in the Roman army. He was a good man, and he was trusted by everyone who knew him. He and his family believed in Jesus, but they didn't know how to become Jesus' disciples.

An angel came to Cornelius as he was praying. The angel said that Cornelius should ask Peter to come and teach him how to become Jesus' disciple. Now, Peter had never taught anyone except Jews before, but an angel told him to go with the men Cornelius had sent.

Peter taught Cornelius and all his family. How glad Peter was to know that God wanted everyone to be disciples of Jesus!